SECURA

Fiona Beddall

LEVEL 2

SCHOLASTIC

Written by: Fiona Beddall
Publisher: Jacquie Bloese
Editor: Sarah Silver
Designer: Dawn Wilson
Picture research: Emma Bree
Photo credits:
Cover: Sutton Motorsport.
Pages 4 & 5: Sutton Motorsport; Business Collection, Sipa/Rex; S. Bruty/Allsport, T. Blackwood/AFP, Time Life/Getty Images; Pingebat/iStockphoto. **Pages 6 & 7:** Sutton Motorsport. **Page 8:** Sipa/Rex. **Page 11:** Sutton Motorsport. **Page 13:** Sutton Motorsport. **Pages 14 & 15:** Sutton Motorsport; P. Rondeau/Allsport/Getty Images; Stockhaus; M. Brown/iStockphoto. **Pages 16 & 17:** D. Alangkara/AFP/Getty Images; M. Brown/iStockphoto. **Pages 18 & 19:** Sutton Motorsport; M. Brown/iStockphoto. **Page 20:** Jones/PA. **Pages 22 & 23:** Sutton Motorsport; STF/AFP/Getty Images. **Pages 24 & 25:** Stockhaus; M. Brown/iStockphoto. **Page 27:** Sutton Motorsport; M. Brown/iStockphoto. **Pages 28 & 29:** Sutton Motorsport. **Pages 30 & 31:** P. Rondeau/Allsport/Getty Images; M. Brown/iStockphoto. **Pages 32 & 33:** Sutton Motorsport; Stockhaus; M. Brown/iStockphoto. **Page 35:** J. M. Loubat/Gamma/Getty Images. **Page 37:** Ase Criadores do Senninha Rogério M. Martins/Ridaut Dias Jr. **Page 39:** G. L. Gautreau/AFP/Getty Images. **Page 41:** G. Giansanti/Corbis; AFP/Getty Images. **Page 43:** P. Le Segretain/Corbis. **Pages 44 & 45:** A. Scorza, M. Cooper/Getty Images. **Pages 46 & 47:** P. Singh/AFP/Getty Images; G. Giansanti/Corbis.
Pages 48 & 49: P. Hertzog, M. Heyhow, R. Rahman/AFP, F. J. Hughes/Fox Photos, R. Riger, Klemantaski Collection, P. Gilham/Getty Images; Stockhaus. **Pages 50 & 51:** C. Knight/Rex; AP/PA; P. Verdy, D. Emmert/AFP/Getty Images, Sutton Motorsport. **Pages 52 & 53:** V. Carnival, S. Franklin/Getty Images; N. Addis/Corbis; M. Schwettmann/iStockphoto.

Published by Scholastic Ltd. 2012

No part of this publication may be reproduced in whole or in part, or stored in a retrieval system, or transmitted in any form or by any means, electronic, mechanical, photocopying, recording or otherwise, without written permission of the publisher. For information regarding permission write to:

Mary Glasgow Magazines (Scholastic Ltd.)
Euston House
24 Eversholt Street
London NW1 1DB

All rights reserved

Printed in Malaysia.
Reprinted in 2014.

CONTENTS

	PAGE
Senna	**4–47**
People and places	**4**
'Second or third place is not enough'	**6**
Chapter 1: Boy racer	**7**
Chapter 2: To Formula One	**12**
Grand Prix races	**16**
Chapter 3: The Lotus years	**17**
Senna's McLaren car	**22**
Chapter 4: Teammate trouble: Senna and Prost	**23**
Chapter 5: 'The James Bond years'	**29**
Chapter 6: Planning the future	**32**
Chapter 7: Senna's last lap	**37**
Chapter 8: After Senna	**43**
Fact Files	**48–53**
Great champions of Formula One	**48**
Famous races	**50**
Brazil	**52**
Self-Study Activities	**54–56**
New Words	**inside back cover**

PEOPLE AND PLACES

AYRTON SENNA

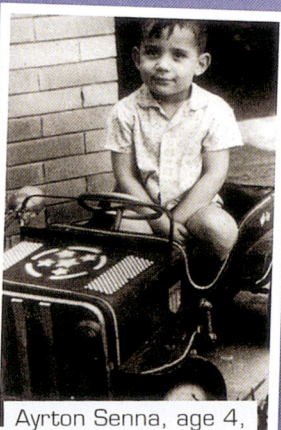

Ayrton in 1984, with his mum and dad, his big sister Viviane and his little brother Leonardo.

Ayrton Senna, age 4, outside his home in São Paulo, Brazil. Cars were already an important part of his life.

Ayrton's wife Lilian, in 1981. They lived in England for a year before Ayrton left her.

Brazilian TV star Xuxa was one of Ayrton's girlfriends.

Alain Prost was Senna's first teammate at McLaren, but they were not friends.

Ayrton's second McLaren teammate, Gerhard Berger, was a close friend.

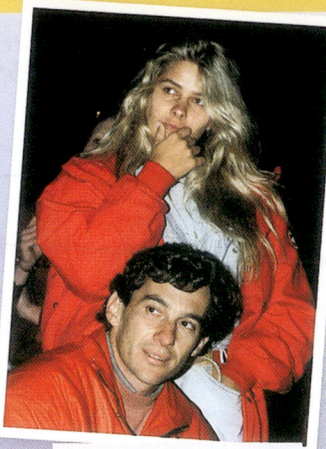

Adriane was Ayrton's girlfriend when he died in 1994.

Ayrton's sister's son, Bruno. Now Bruno also races in Formula One.

PLACES

São Paulo: Ayrton grew up in a nice part of this Brazilian city, but many people there have very difficult lives.

The race track: Every year, drivers race in the Formula One World Championship on race tracks around the world.

AYRTON SENNA
'Second or third place is not enough'

After ten years as a Formula One driver, the San Marino Grand Prix* was a race that Ayrton Senna knew well. It was 1994, and he was hoping for his fourth win on the course. But on the seventh lap, his car left the track at 306 kilometres an hour and crashed into a wall. Senna was dead.

Millions of people were watching the race on TV on that terrible day, as motor racing lost its biggest star. When Senna died at the age of thirty-four, he was one of the most exciting and popular drivers in Formula One.

He was the winner of forty-one Grand Prix races and three world championships. He always drove fast on a dry track. When it was wet, no one could beat him. For many people, he was the greatest driver that ever lived. And in his homeland, Brazil, he was more than a driver. He was a man who brought hope to his people.

* The Grand Prix is the name of any race in the Formula One motor racing championship

CHAPTER 1
Boy racer

Ayrton Senna da Silva was born on March the 21st, 1960, in the city of São Paulo, Brazil. He was the middle child in the family. His sister Viviane was two years older, and his brother Leonardo a few years younger. They called him 'Beco'.

There were many millions of very poor Brazilians, but the da Silvas were rich. Beco's father, Milton, owned a business that had a thousand workers. It made car parts and sold soft drinks. Milton da Silva also owned a lot of land. The family lived in a big house and had a very comfortable life.

By the age of three, Beco had a little car. He loved it so much that his father built him a go-kart with a small engine for his fourth birthday. The little boy spent all his time on the go-kart and he could control it well. Beco started dreaming of a future as a racing driver.

Three years later, his father had a big surprise. He saw Beco driving a full-size car across a field! Even with his little legs, the boy was controlling the car well and changing gear – a very difficult job. In the end, Milton could not be angry.

Milton was less happy when, at the age of eight, Beco got in trouble with the police. He was driving the family car on the city streets.

Beco wasn't very interested in school work, but he worked hard. He wanted to please his parents. Then he could spend the rest of his time at the go-kart track.

At the age of eight, he was in races with people twice his age. They could turn corners better, but he was much lighter than them. Because of this, his go-kart could go much faster. He loved the races, and his parents enjoyed them too. When Beco was ten, they bought him a better, faster go-kart.

Ayrton, age 13, at a go-kart race with his father

* * *

Motor racing was growing more popular in Brazil at this time. Formula One racer Emerson Fittipaldi came from São Paulo, and in 1972 he became Brazil's first world champion. A year later, São Paulo held its first Grand Prix.

That same year, Milton da Silva asked Lucio Pascual Gascon to watch his son on the track. Pascual (or 'Tchê') was Fittipaldi's engineer when the famous driver was racing go-karts in São Paulo. 'Your son's going to win lots of races,' Tchê told Milton. He agreed to build engines for Ayrton's go-karts.

Soon Ayrton was spending a lot of time in Tchê's workrooms. He learnt everything that he could from this brilliant engineer. Later, he knew more about engineering than any other driver in Formula One.

Ayrton won a lot of go-kart races, and he hated to lose. Once, on a very rainy day, he lost control of his go-kart and finished last. After that, when he saw rain clouds in the sky, he always hurried to the race track. He drove thousands of laps in wet weather. This practice helped him a lot in Formula One – no one was faster than Senna in the rain.

* * *

At the age of sixteen Senna was go-kart champion of Brazil, and at seventeen he was champion of all South America. When he was eighteen, Senna went to Italy. He could speak very little Italian and no other language except Portuguese. But when he drove, he didn't need language. By the end of his first day there, he was finishing his laps faster than the world champion who was practising on the same track. He came sixth in the go-kart world championship in France two weeks later.

After that, he went home to Brazil. There he finished school and started a course in business studies. He continued to race go-karts, and returned to Europe in 1979 and 1980 for the world championships. Both times he finished second.

* * *

His father wanted Ayrton to join the family business, but Ayrton had other ideas. He was twenty now, and he wanted to race cars, not go-karts. For that, he needed to live in England.

England was a great place for motor racing. The top drivers raced in Formula One, but many of them learnt their driving in England's Formula Ford 1600, Formula Ford 2000 and Formula Three. The Van Diemen team needed a driver to race in Formula Ford 1600, and they were interested in Senna. But there was one problem. Motor racing cost a lot of money. Van Diemen didn't pay their drivers. Instead, the drivers had to pay them. Milton da Silva wasn't sure that his son was doing the right thing. But in the end he agreed to pay for Ayrton's racing.

* * *

Ayrton had a nineteen-year-old girlfriend in Brazil: Lilian. They were friends as young children, and now they were in love. After only two months together, they decided to get married. The day after they became husband and wife, they flew to England.

Like Ayrton, Lilian came from a rich family. Now, for the first time in her life, she had to do housework. The weather in England seemed terribly cold and they didn't speak much English. Life wasn't easy.

Senna spent most of his time on the race track. He had a lot to learn. In go-kart racing, the tracks were always flat. Now he had to drive on hills too. But he was a fast learner.

In his first race, he came fifth. The next week, he came third. And the week after that, it was raining. After years of practice in the rain of São Paulo, no one could beat him on a wet track. He won the race.

Ayrton and Lilian in England in 1981

The rest of the season continued to go well. He finished first in twelve of the twenty races. At the end of the season, he seemed to have a great future in motor racing. It was a big surprise when he told everyone, 'I won't be here next year. I'm stopping racing.'

The main problem was money. His father didn't want to pay for a second year in England. Ayrton also knew that his wife was unhappy in England. She wasn't very interested in motor racing and she had no friends in England. 'I was his second love,' she said later. 'His first love was always racing.' She really wanted to go home.

Milton da Silva still wanted his son to work with him. Ayrton decided to go back to Brazil and study business in São Paulo again. It was time to forget his dreams.

CHAPTER 2
To Formula One

For five months, Senna tried to live in São Paulo without motor racing. But he couldn't do it. His father finally understood that his future wasn't in the family business. In February 1982, Ayrton left Lilian and returned to England.

His father helped him with money again, and he now had a little help from some businesses too. They gave him money, and he put their names on his car.

In the 1982 season he raced in Formula Ford 2000. The cars were harder to drive than the Formula Ford 1600 cars of the year before. Senna didn't have much practice time before the start of the season, but he still won his first race by almost ten seconds. He was easily the best driver in Formula Ford that year. He won twenty-three of his thirty races.

After this some good teams asked Senna to join them. They wanted him to race in Formula Three the next year, and perhaps in Formula One the year after that. Senna wasn't interested in a 'perhaps'. He said no to them all. No one offered him a car in Formula One for the next year, so he chose to drive for the best team in Formula Three: West Surrey Racing.

* * *

After a few months at home in Brazil, Senna started the 1983 Formula Three season with nine easy wins. He even won when he was ill. No one could remember a better driver in Formula Three. But then things started to go wrong. A British driver, Martin Brundle, won the tenth race because Senna's car had the wrong tyres for the weather. Brundle's car also had a better engine. After this, Brundle was hard to beat. Because of all Senna's wins at the start of the season, a second place in the rest of the races could make him the champion. But Senna didn't like to be second. Instead, in race after race, he tried everything to overtake Brundle. He often crashed. 'In one race,' remembers Brundle, 'he drove his car right on top of mine. I couldn't get out of the car until they moved his car away.'

Senna's car on top of Brundle's car

Finally there was just one more race in the season. With a win in this last race, Brundle could win the championship. Senna drove all the way to Italy to get a better engine for his car. It made a difference. In the race, Senna was in front from the start and won easily. He was the 1983 Formula Three champion.

* * *

Now Senna needed to find a team for Formula One. He was clearly a brilliant driver and a lot of teams were interested in him. But each team could only have two drivers in Formula One, and most of them already had two good drivers. In the end, Senna had to drive for Toleman, a team with some of the slowest cars in Formula One.

His first Grand Prix, at home in Brazil, was terrible. There was a problem with the engine, and he couldn't even finish the race. But then, even with the car's bad tyres and slow engine, Senna's results got better.

In May 1984, there was a special race at the Nürburgring in Germany for past, present and future champions of Formula One. Everyone had to drive in exactly the same car: an ordinary Mercedes road car. Senna was not a famous driver, so no one invited him. But he really wanted to race against these great champions. He spoke to a friend who worked at Mercedes. In the end, Mercedes allowed him into the race. He drove brilliantly and won.

Senna driving a Mercedes saloon car at the Nürburgring in 1984

That weekend, many famous drivers from the past were talking about Senna for the first time. But the bosses of Mercedes were upset. The winner's car went into their car museum in Stuttgart. 'But who will want to see the car of this nobody?' they asked.

THE MONACO GRAND PRIX 1984

Senna's best Formula One race that year was in Monaco. He qualified in thirteenth position, on a dry track. But the main race was in the rain. After twenty laps, he was in second place, with French driver Alain Prost half a minute ahead of him. By the end of lap thirty-one, the difference was only 7.4 seconds. There were a lot more laps. Senna felt sure that he could win.

But the rain was heavy now. The boss of the track decided to end the race early. A red flag went up. Senna moved into first place as he and Prost crossed the line at the end of lap thirty-two. This was Senna's first Grand Prix win, and he was really happy. But a few moments later he learnt his mistake. The end of the race was lap thirty-one, not lap thirty-two. Prost was the winner.

Many people were angry about the result. 'The rain wasn't too bad,' they said. Prost was French, and the people of Monaco loved French drivers. Did the race end early because they wanted Prost as their winner? Senna didn't say anything. He knew that all the talk about the race in the newspapers was good for his future.

The Monaco Grand Prix race goes through the town

GRAND PRIX RACES

During the racing season today (usually March to November), there are about twenty Grand Prix races, although in Senna's day there were only sixteen.

Counting down to race day

Monday and Tuesday: People from the different teams arrive at the race track. They put up motorhomes and garages for the drivers, engineers and cars.

Wednesday: The racing cars arrive in pieces. The engineers put them together.

Thursday: Engineers check the cars carefully. The drivers and the TV and newspaper people arrive.

Friday and Saturday: The drivers practise on the track and sometimes ask the engineers for changes to the cars. Then they drive laps as fast as possible.

The person with the fastest lap gets 'pole position': he starts in front in the race on Sunday. The person with the second fastest lap starts second, etc.

Sunday: This is race day. The race takes about one and a half hours, or longer in bad weather. Drivers can stop at the pits so that the engineers can work on the cars. Drivers get points if they finish in the front ten, with most points for the winner. The person with the highest number of points at the end of the season wins the championship.

....
What do these words mean?
You can use a dictionary.
check   motorhome
....

16

CHAPTER 3
The Lotus years

Senna's first year in Formula One with the Toleman team included some good results. He ended the season in ninth place. But he wasn't happy with the Toleman cars. When Peter Warr, the Lotus boss, offered him a car for the 1985 season, he took it. After a few months in Brazil for the European winter, Senna moved back to England to join the Lotus team. His teammate was Elio de Angelis.

From the start, Warr and his engineers knew that the young man from Brazil was something special. He learnt quickly how his engine worked. He then made careful plans with the engineers so that it could work even better. He practised harder than any other driver that they knew. When he was driving, there was nothing in his head except his car. He clearly wanted to become the best in the world. And most people agreed that he could do it.

THE PORTUGUESE GRAND PRIX 1985

This was the second race of the season, and it rained heavily. Senna was ahead from the start. He was winning by twelve seconds after ten laps, and by thirty seconds after twenty laps. But he couldn't see very far in front. The track was much more dangerous than in Monaco the year before. At one moment he lost control and all four wheels were on the grass. But he was lucky. He got the car back onto the track and finished the race a full minute before the driver in second place. It was his first Grand Prix win, and it felt fantastic.

No one could beat Senna in the rain

* * *

Suddenly people thought that Senna could win this year's championship. But he had a lot of bad luck with the car. In Italy and England, he used all his fuel before the end of the race. In Monaco, South Africa and Australia, the engine stopped working.

Alain Prost won the championship, and Senna finished fourth. 'Senna is a star of the future,' said lots of people in Formula One. 'Perhaps 1986 will be his big year.'

* * *

The 1986 season started quite well, with a second place in Rio de Janeiro. And the race after that was one of the most exciting that Formula One has ever seen.

THE SPANISH GRAND PRIX 1986

The British driver Nigel Mansell was a long way in front of the other drivers. He was having a good race. But then he started going slower because he needed new tyres. Ten laps before the finish, Senna moved into first place. Mansell's only hope was to change his tyres. He stopped at the pits. Senna went twenty seconds ahead. But Senna's tyres were old too, and Mansell had fast, new tyres now. At the start of the last lap, Mansell was only 1.5 seconds behind Senna. He just needed to overtake. But Senna didn't let him. He drove from one side of the track to the other to keep Mansell behind him. In the last moments, Mansell was starting to move in front. But it was too late. Senna crossed the line first, by just 0.014 seconds. He had a third Grand Prix win.

* * *

The next few races were not as good for Senna, and then there was terrible news. Elio de Angelis, Senna's teammate the year before, crashed his car during practice. The car caught fire. Some drivers tried to help him, but they couldn't get him out for a long time. He died later that day. Senna and everyone else in Formula One were very upset.

In the thirty years between 1952 and 1982, Formula One lost forty-four drivers. After that it became safer because of changes in car engineering. But driving round a race track at more than 300 kilometres an hour could never be really safe.

The racing season continued. Senna usually did well in the qualifying laps, but in races the Lotus car's engine needed too much fuel. Senna couldn't drive it as hard as he wanted.

He qualified first at the Detroit Grand Prix. As soon

as he finished his last qualifying lap on the Saturday, he hurried back to the TV in his hotel room. Brazil was playing an important game in the football World Cup.*

They lost. But the next day, Senna won his race, and drove another lap with a Brazilian flag. His country's football team was having problems, but in motor racing Brazil had a winner.

After this, Senna always waved the Brazilian flag when he won. He also had the flag colours, green and yellow, on his helmet. The people of Brazil loved him for it.

* * *

Senna ended the 1986 season fourth, as he did the year before. Now it was time for a holiday. Ayrton returned to Brazil but he spoke often to the Lotus team. They had a better engine for next year. Everyone had great hopes for the next season.

When the races of 1987 started, their hopes soon disappeared. The new engine was good, but the body

* The World Cup happens every four years. The best footballing countries in the world play in it.

of their new car was slow and heavy. With Senna at the wheel, there were some brilliant results, but the faster Williams cars were better. Senna came third in the championship.

For Senna, this wasn't good enough. He decided to leave Lotus and race for McLaren in the 1988 season. There was a lot of money in Formula One now. McLaren offered him about $7.5 million a year.

Ayrton moved his main home from England to Monaco. With more money, he could fly home to Brazil more often. His money also allowed him to help people in Brazil. He started to give a lot of money to his country's poorest children, and to hospitals.

During his months in Brazil that year, he met Xuxa. Xuxa was one of the most famous people in the country. At the age of twenty-four, she starred in her own TV show and was a very popular singer. One day Senna phoned her at work, and they soon agreed to meet. He drove to Xuxa's house and they talked and talked. As he left, her dog followed him to his car. 'This dog knows that I'm good for you,' he laughed.

But he had to be back in Europe soon. Xuxa was also very busy with her work. They both knew that they couldn't be together ... yet.

* * *

Senna's teammate at McLaren was Alain Prost, the 1985 and 1986 champion. Senna didn't know Prost well, and asked other drivers about him. 'At McLaren, he's number one,' said a friend of Senna's. 'You'll have to learn his way of working.'

Senna didn't agree. He planned to make Prost the number two.

SENNA'S MCLAREN CAR

In Formula One, the speed of the cars around corners is hard to believe. Why don't they fly off the track? The answer is 'downforce'. When the car moves, air goes over it. The air pushes the car down onto the track. Because of downforce, a Formula One car today can drive up a wall if it is going fast enough!

This is the back wing. It helps to push the back tyres down onto the track.

This high bit in the centre of the car keeps the driver safe if the car lands the wrong way up.

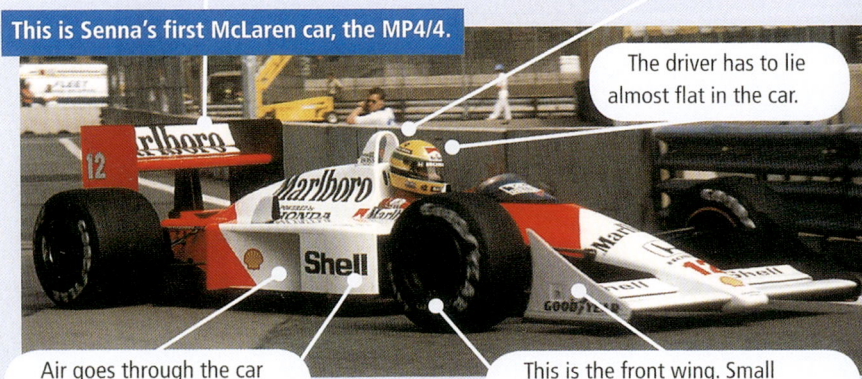

This is Senna's first McLaren car, the MP4/4.

The driver has to lie almost flat in the car.

Air goes through the car and out of this hole. It helps to keep the engine cool.

This is the front wing. Small changes to its shape can change the car's speed around corners.

The engine, a Honda V6 1500cc turbo, is in the centre of the car. There are six gears.

There's a brake on each wheel, and these become red hot in a race.

The car is 4.39 metres long and 540 kilos. (A small car for a family is about the same length but more than twice as heavy.)

What do these words mean? You can use a dictionary.
air   brake   shape   speed
turbo   wing

CHAPTER 4
Teammate trouble: Senna and Prost

In his first season at McLaren, Senna finally had the car of his dreams. It had the best engine and the best body in Formula One. Senna's hands hurt terribly when he was driving the Lotus. In his new car, driving was easy. The McLaren team also had good people working for them.

The engineers at McLaren loved working with Senna. He worked as hard as they did and he always thanked them at the end of a long day. And, unlike other drivers, he always said when a problem was his own fault, not the car's.

* * *

Senna and his new teammate Alain Prost

At first, Prost and Senna worked quite well as teammates. But they were very different. Prost thought carefully about a race. He did exactly as much as he needed to. If he could win a championship with a third place in the race, he came third.

Senna could never do that. 'Something inside me, something very strong, pushes me on,' he once explained. 'I try to beat myself.'

He also tried to beat Prost. As they now drove in the same cars, the races were a fair test of their driving. Senna drove the fastest qualifying lap in thirteen of the season's sixteen races. But qualifying laps didn't win races. Senna drove his car so hard that there were sometimes problems.

* * *

Monaco was the third Grand Prix of the season. While he was qualifying, Senna drove better than ever before. He was excited about the main race on Sunday. Monaco was one of his favourite tracks.

THE MONACO GRAND PRIX 1988

The race started, and soon Senna was far ahead of Prost and the other drivers. The McLaren boss, Ron Dennis, told him to slow down now. Senna was going to win anyway, he said. But going slower wasn't easy for Senna. Eleven laps before the end of the race, he crashed into the side of the track. Prost drove past and won the Grand Prix.

Senna jumped angrily out of his car and went to his flat. He didn't speak to anyone. Hours later, he was still crying. 'I made a mistake,' he said later. 'I became much stronger after that.'

* * *

By the time of the Portuguese Grand Prix, Senna had seven wins and Prost had four. During the race, Prost tried to overtake Senna near the pits. Senna drove to Prost's side of the track. Prost had almost no track to drive on. His car touched the pit wall. An accident here could kill not only the drivers but also the engineers on the other side of the wall ... but luckily the accident didn't happen. Prost won the race in the end, but he wasn't happy. 'It was dangerous,' he said. 'If Senna wants the world championship as much as that, he can have it.'

Prost and Senna could not be friends after this. Prost won again in Spain. He now had five wins against Senna's seven, with only two more races in the season. Prost had to win in Japan and Australia. Senna only had to win one of those races. Then he could finally be world champion.

THE JAPANESE GRAND PRIX 1988

At the start of the race, Senna made a stupid mistake. His engine stopped just as the race was starting. Luckily for Senna, the track went downhill and he could start his engine again. But he was now in fourteenth place and Prost was in front. By the end of the fourth lap, Senna was fourth. Then it started to rain. Prost drove slower, and Senna overtook him. The race ended with Senna in first place and Prost in second place. Senna was world champion!

* * *

Later he told the newspapers about the end of the race. 'I saw God,' he said. Some people laughed at him. Prost said to the newspapers, 'Ayrton has a small problem. He thinks he can't kill himself because he believes in God. I think that's very dangerous for the other drivers.'

Senna was angry. 'Yes, I believe in God. But that doesn't mean that I can't die.' After de Angelis's death, he knew the dangers of motor racing as well as anyone.

* * *

Soon the season was over and Senna went home to Brazil as world champion. There were parties with lots of important people, but his friends were still the old friends, from school and from go-kart racing. He was very close to his family, too. But the most important person in his life at this time was Xuxa.

Senna bought his own home in Brazil: a beach house at Angra. He and Xuxa planned to spend as much time as possible there. Of course, with their busy lives it wasn't easy. But Senna loved her deeply. He hoped to have children with her in the future.

* * *

When Senna went back to Europe for the 1989 season, the problems with Prost started again.

Like last year, the two McLaren cars were the fastest in Formula One. Senna qualified first in thirteen of the sixteen races that season. Prost wasn't happy. He told the newspapers that his and Senna's cars had different engines. But it wasn't true. The two engines were exactly the same.

Senna was faster, but he had more problems with his car. Sometimes he drove it too hard because he hated being in second place. When Senna didn't finish a race, Prost usually won. And Prost got points in a lot of races for finishing second. By the time of the Japanese Grand Prix, Prost had more points. Senna had to win both of the last races of the season to become champion.

Senna was very popular all around the world

THE JAPANESE GRAND PRIX 1989

In Japan, the two McLaren teammates drove brilliantly. For a long time, they were close together, with Prost just ahead. On the forty-seventh lap, Senna tried to overtake. Prost turned into the next corner early, with Senna next to him. The two cars touched and lost control. They drove slowly off the track together.

Both men thought for a moment. If they didn't finish the race, Prost was world champion. Prost got out of the car. But Senna turned his car round and drove to the pits. The engineers did some quick work on the car, and then he returned to the track. He drove an amazing race and crossed the finish line first. He could still win the world championship!

But there was a problem. While Senna was racing, Prost was talking to the head of FISA*, Frenchman Jean-Marie Balestre. They spoke the same language, and were good friends. Now, after the race, Balestre decided to disqualify Senna. Senna didn't drive the whole course, he said. He left the track during the crash and joined it again at a different place. Senna got no points for the race, and Prost was world champion.

* FISA is short for the *Fédération Internationale du Sport Automobile*. It controlled Formula One and other racing championships.

Prost talking to Balestre

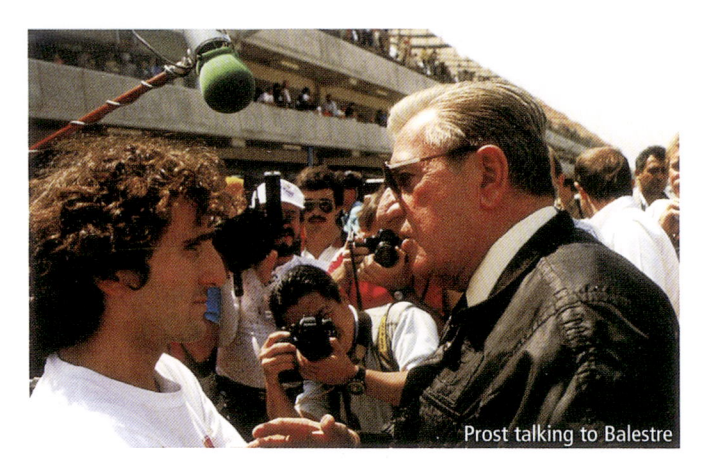

Senna was very angry. Other people sometimes left the track in a race and joined it in a different place. Balestre didn't disqualify them.

Disqualifying Senna seemed completely unfair. Senna and Ron Dennis asked FISA to think again. But Balestre didn't want to listen. Prost was still the world champion.

CHAPTER 5
'The James Bond years'

After the last race of the 1989 season, Senna returned to Brazil. He started exercising very hard. He ran about twenty kilometres every day. Everyone knew that you could control a Formula One car better with strong arms. But Senna thought that your whole body had to be strong for the most difficult Grand Prix races. This was quite a new idea at the time, but now all Formula One drivers do a lot of exercise.

During his time in Brazil, Senna wanted to spend time with Xuxa. But she was still very busy with work. They were in love, but could they ever be truly happy together? She wanted her boyfriend with her in São Paulo. He had to be in Europe, and wanted his girlfriend with him at his races. In 1990, they sadly agreed that their love was impossible.

* * *

Senna had a lot of friends in Formula One: his engineers, the track doctor Sid Watkins, and many others. But he wasn't usually friends with the other drivers. He had to beat them. He didn't want to beat his friends.

His new teammate at McLaren was Gerhard Berger from Austria. Berger hoped to beat Senna in lots of races, but that didn't happen. Berger started to understand that Senna was a better driver – the number one at McLaren, and in all of Formula One. Slowly Senna and he became friends. The two men were the same age and had the same ideas about life.

'Ayrton was the best friend that I ever had in Formula One,' said Berger later. He talks about their years as friends as 'the James Bond years'. They had money, beautiful women, and fast cars. Life was a lot of fun.

Senna and Gerhard Berger were good friends

* * *

After fourteen races in the 1990 season, Senna had six wins. There was only one other person who could possibly become the 1990 champion: Ferrari's new driver,

Alain Prost. The next race was the Japanese Grand Prix. Like the year before, it could decide the championship. But there was one difference. This time Prost had to win the race to win the championship.

THE JAPANESE GRAND PRIX 1990

In 1988 and 1989, the fastest qualifier started the main race on the right of the track. But most drivers thought that you could start the race faster from the left. Before this race the track bosses agreed to have the starting place on the left for the fastest qualifier. Senna then drove the fastest qualifying lap. Prost was in second place. But later they heard Balestre's orders for the race. Senna had to start on the right, and Prost on the left. Senna was very angry.

Prost started quicker in the race, because he was on the better part of the track. He and Senna both tried to take the fastest line around the first corner. They crashed and went off the track. For both drivers, it was the end of the race.

Senna had the most points of the season, so he was world champion. Prost was very angry. 'He saw that my car was better. So he pushed me out,' said Prost. Senna disagreed. He didn't think that the crash was his fault. But for both drivers it was a terrible end to the championship.

Around the world, people were upset. Important people in France asked FISA not to give the championship to Senna. They wanted a season with no winner, because Senna was a bad example for the sport of motor racing.

But this year FISA didn't disqualify Senna. He was world champion for the second time.

CHAPTER 6
Planning the future

Back in Brazil after the end of the 1990 season, Senna started planning his future as a businessman. He bought a tall building in São Paulo as his office. He started wearing t-shirts with a special 'S' sign on them. He planned to put this sign on all the things that his business sold.

The 1991 season started with a win for Senna in the USA. The race after that was in Brazil. Every year, Senna seemed to have bad luck at the Brazilian Grand Prix. This year he really wanted to win.

THE BRAZILIAN GRAND PRIX 1991

Senna started in front, and by the fiftieth lap he was far ahead of the other drivers. But suddenly there was a problem with his gearbox. He could only drive in sixth gear. It was raining, and in sixth gear corners were almost impossible. His arms hurt badly. He wanted to stop, but the Brazilians really wanted a home win for Senna. Could he keep the car going to the end of the race?

Yes, he could! Senna crossed the line first. He couldn't hold the Brazilian flag because of his tired arms. But finally, after eight tries and with his people watching, he was the winner of the Brazilian Grand Prix. 'God gave me this race,' he said later.

* * *

By the time of the Japanese Grand Prix, Senna only needed a second place to win the championship. He was in front for most of the race. Just before the end he slowed

Senna at the front in the 1991 Brazilian Grand Prix

down so his friend and teammate Berger could cross the finish line first.

Senna was now world champion for the third time. At the end of the race, he kept his helmet on his head. He didn't want to show everyone that he was crying. He was crying because he was happy, of course. But he was also thinking about the last two Japanese Grand Prix and his problems with Prost and Balestre.

* * *

During the European winter, Ayrton was in Brazil, at his country home near São Paulo. It now had a new go-kart track. Ayrton and his sister's eight-year-old son,

Bruno, loved racing on it. One day, there was a go-kart race for lots of Brazilian children. Ayrton waved the flag at the finish line and joked with the kids. Bruno won the race, and his uncle was very happy. Later he told the newspapers, 'You think I'm fast? Wait until you see Bruno!'

* * *

The 1992 season was a bad one for Senna. The McLaren cars were too slow that year. Williams cars had better engines and more computer controls than before. They made a big difference.

Senna's best win that year was in Monaco, after some exciting laps with Mansell right behind him. He only won two other races and came fourth in the championship.

But at the Belgian Grand Prix Senna did something much more important than winning a race. The French driver Érik Comas had a bad crash during a qualifying lap. Senna was just behind him. He stopped his car. Then he hurried across the track – he didn't think about the danger. From Sid Watkins, the Formula One doctor, Senna knew what to do in an accident. He turned off Comas's engine so a fire couldn't start. When the doctors arrived, Senna was holding Comas in exactly the right way. Comas believes that Senna saved his life that day.

* * *

Berger and Senna didn't want another year at McLaren, in a car that wasn't good enough. Berger moved to Ferrari for 1993, but Senna wanted to race for Williams. There was just one problem. Prost was planning to race for Williams too. And Prost was clear that he and Senna couldn't be teammates again.

Senna found out very late that he couldn't move to

Williams. And he had no job offers from other teams. He almost gave up motor racing completely. But when the new Formula One season started, he had to be part of it. He decided to drive in the first Grand Prix for McLaren. But he only wanted to drive for them in other races if their car was good enough.

He was surprised. The McLaren's engine wasn't great. But the car had the same computer controls that the Williams cars had in 1992. It was a nice drive.

He came second in the first race, in South Africa. Then it was the Brazilian Grand Prix, and he won. In the next race, in England, he probably drove the best first lap of his life. He started in fourth place, and fell back to fifth at the start. But in heavy rain he overtook the four cars ahead of him in just one lap, and then continued to an easy win.

After this race, he went back to Brazil. He had a new girlfriend, nineteen-year-old Adriane. Senna was deeply in love. After two more races, both wins for Prost, Adriane flew out to be with him in Monaco. She chose her race well: Senna won his sixth Grand Prix on the track.

Ayrton with his new girlfriend Adriane

season. He didn't want to come back to Brazil between races. It seemed that Adriane was taking Ayrton away from them.

* * *

Formula One was less dangerous now than in the 1960s and 70s. Drivers wore clothes that kept them safe in a fire. The cars were stronger and there was even a hospital at each Grand Prix track.

But motor racing could never be completely safe. Accidents – bad accidents – were still a part of Formula One.

The new computer controls made cars safer, but many people didn't agree with them. Senna couldn't decide. He wanted the new electronics in his car, because cars without them were slower. But he worried that a brilliant driver and an OK driver could get the same results in a car with computer controls. There was also the problem of money. These electronics were very expensive, so only the richest Formula One teams could have them. He wanted a championship that was fair for all the drivers.

The FIA* decided that, for the 1994 season, no cars could have computer controls. This was very bad news for Senna's new team Williams, and for the other teams that used computer controls. The engineers didn't have long to change the cars. They were still as fast as before but, without their electronics, they were very difficult to control. 'It's going to be a season with lots of accidents,' said Senna.

No one listened. In 1994, there was no Prost and no Mansell. Senna was the only past champion still in Formula One and in the last few years Williams cars were

---

* FIA is short for the *Fédération Internationale de l'Automobile*. FISA changed to FIA in 1993, and since then it has controlled Formula One.

the best on the track. Everyone thought that Senna could win the championship. But a young driver from Germany, Michael Schumacher, won the first two races of the season in a Benetton car (Benetton bought the Toleman team in 1986). Senna didn't finish either race.

San Marino was the track for the next Grand Prix, and Williams did a lot of work on Senna's car before the race. Senna's first qualifying laps at San Marino were fast. But after only fifteen minutes, there was news of an accident. Rubens Barrichello was driving round a corner when his car hit the side of the track. The car flew into a wall of tyres and landed the wrong way up.

Barrichello was a young driver from São Paulo. When Senna heard about the accident, he went to the track hospital. He spoke to Sid Watkins. Luckily there was nothing badly wrong with Barrichello. He woke up a few moments later and saw Senna's face above him. Senna was crying.

Senna talking to Sid Watkins

Then Senna went back to his car. He drove the fastest lap of the Grand Prix weekend. But he still wasn't happy about the car. He gave his engineers a long list of things to work on.

Soon there was another accident. An Austrian driver, Roland Ratzenberger, was driving in his second Grand Prix. He crashed into a wall at 315 kilometres an hour. Sid Watkins and the other doctors were there 25 seconds later.

Senna saw the accident on TV. It looked bad. Senna went to the track hospital for the second time in two days. Sid told him the sad news: Ratzenberger was dead.

Senna didn't want to drive any more qualifying laps. Ratzenberger's death was the first in Formula One for seven years and all the drivers were very upset. They planned to meet together before the next Grand Prix in Monaco. They wanted to talk about making Formula One safer.

That night Ayrton spoke on the phone to Adriane. At first he decided not to race the next day. But then he decided that it was better to race. He wanted to carry an Austrian flag in his car. Then he could wave it when he won, for Ratzenberger.

The next day Alain Prost was at the track. Normally Senna didn't speak to Prost, but today he sat down with him for some breakfast. They talked like old friends about making Formula One less dangerous.

Soon it was time for the race. Senna was starting in front. He looked across quickly at Gerhard Berger and smiled. Then, at exactly two o'clock, the cars drove off towards the first corner.

Two cars crashed right at the start, so the race stopped. Luckily, no one was hurt. The other cars continued slowly behind a special car, while people cleared the crash from

Senna before his final race at the San Marino Grand Prix

the track. At three fifteen, the race started again. Two minutes later, Senna was going into the Tamburello corner. There was a big wall there, only a few metres from the track. At the corner, Senna's car didn't turn. It went off the track at 305 kilometres an hour and hit the wall.

Sid Watkins reached the place of the accident a minute later. He did all the usual things for a driver. But there were deep holes in Senna's head. Sid knew that he was dying.

People could see from the TV pictures that it was a very bad accident. But at the track, only a few people knew this. The FIA wanted the Grand Prix to continue. The race started again and Schumacher won.

Then everyone heard that Senna was dying in hospital. In Portugal, Adriane got onto a plane. She was still hoping that the accident wasn't too bad. But before the plane left, she had a phone call from the hospital. Senna was dead.

CHAPTER 8
After Senna

Brazilian schools and offices closed on the day that Senna's body came home to Brazil. About three million people stood in the streets of São Paulo to see him one last time.

There was a green and yellow flag over the box that held his body. It was the Brazilian flag that he always waved after a Grand Prix win. On the top of the flag was his famous green and yellow helmet. At Ibirapuera Park, the Senna family had some quiet moments with him. And then it was the turn of the ordinary people of Brazil. They waited in the park, in a line five kilometres long. Over the next seven hours, they walked slowly past Senna's body and said goodbye.

Adriane came, with many of Senna's friends from Formula One: Ron Dennis, Frank Williams, Gerhard Berger, Rubens Barrichello. Prost came too – a friend at last. But the bosses of Formula One stayed away. Senna's family didn't want them there. They were upset that the racing at San Marino continued after Ayrton's accident.

Younger people had three colours on their faces: green and yellow for Brazil, and black for death. There were messages everywhere: 'Thank you, Senna.' They wanted to thank him for the exciting Sundays of Formula One on TV, and for bringing hope back to Brazil. 'He was the one good thing in this country,' one person said.

São Paulo, 1994

* * *

There was still a big question that needed an answer: why did Senna's accident happen? No one really knew. A few people thought that he just made a mistake. More people thought that some of the car's controls stopped working. Others thought that Senna's car hit something on the track – perhaps part of a car from the earlier accident that day.

Frank Williams and his engineers felt very upset. They lost a dear friend on the track at San Marino. And perhaps his death was their fault. The Williams team had to answer a lot of questions. Thirteen years after the accident, the police finally decided that Senna's death was the fault of the Williams engineers. But many people still don't agree.

Drivers remember Senna at the Belgian Grand Prix in August, 1994

There was another question, too. Why were there no tyres in front of the hard wall on the Tamburello corner? Everyone knew that it was a dangerous corner. In just seven years, four drivers had accidents there, including Gerhard Berger. But Senna and others thought that tyre walls could be dangerous. A car could hit the tyres and fly back onto the track in front of other drivers. Now walls like this all have tyres on them.

Many other changes came after Senna's and Ratzenberger's deaths. Formula One cars had to have slower engines. They had to have more crash tests before they could race. And the Grand Prix tracks had to change their most dangerous corners. Since that terrible weekend

FACT FILE

BRAZIL

Brazil is the largest country in South America and the fifth largest in the world. More than 190 million people live there.

Cities

São Paulo is Brazil's biggest city, home to almost 20 million people. But Brazil's most famous city is Rio de Janeiro. It has beautiful beaches like Ipanema and Copacabana. It also holds a world-famous Carnival every February or March.

Language

Brazilians speak Portuguese because for three hundred years Brazil was a colony of Portugal. It is the only country in South America where Portuguese is the main language.

The dictatorship

From 1964, Brazil was under a dictatorship. It was dangerous to ask for changes in Brazil. The dictatorship killed a lot of its enemies. It put others in prison or sent them away from their homeland. The dictatorship ended in 1985 and the first true election for many years was in 1989.

Favelas

In the 1970s, many Brazilians moved to big cities like São Paulo and Rio de Janeiro, but there weren't enough homes for everyone. The poor built their own little homes on the hills outside the cities. People called these groups of homes *favelas*. More than 11 million Brazilians still live in favelas today. Life is very difficult there.

Rich and poor

There is a very big difference between the lives of rich people and poor people in Brazil. Lots of people are so rich that they travel around by helicopter, not car. But millions of children live on the streets, with little food and little hope of a happy future.

....
: **What do these words mean?** :
: **You can use a dictionary.** :
: **colony   helicopter   dictatorship** :
: **enemy   prison   election** :
....

Football

There are few people who haven't heard of the great Brazilian football players Pelé, Ronaldo and Ronaldinho. Brazil has won the World Cup five times, more than any other country. But while Senna was racing in Formula One, the Brazilian team was never even in the top four in the World Cup. Brazil really needed a new sports star. That star was Senna.

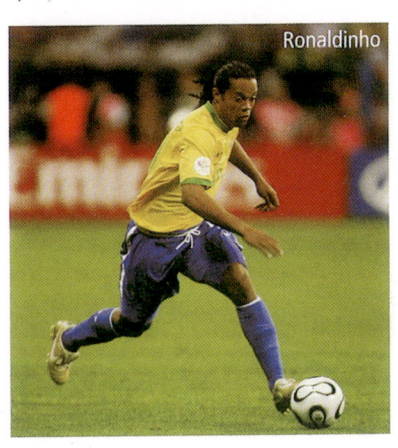

Ronaldinho

SELF-STUDY ACTIVITIES

CHAPTERS 1-3

Before you read

You can use your dictionary for these questions.

1 Use these words to complete the sentences.
   **beat championship control go-kart
   lap overtake qualify race season track**
   a) My .... is fast, but it crashes a lot because I can't .... it.
   b) At the end of the football ...., Chelsea won the ....
   c) The two fastest runners in this .... will .... for the Olympics.
   d) I drove one .... around the .... in a racing car. It was cool!
   e) You have to .... the other drivers if you want to .... them.

2 Which things are parts of a car? Why do people need the other things at a motor race?
   engine flag gear pit tyre

After you read

3 Put the sentences in the correct order.
   a) He decided to stop racing.
   b) Ayrton's father gave him his first go-kart.
   c) He got married.
   d) He became the champion of Formula Three.
   e) He went to race in Italy.
   f) He drove a full-size car for the first time.
   g) He moved to England.

4 Are these sentences true or false? Correct the false sentences.
   a) Ayrton came from a poor family in Brazil.
   b) Ayrton got a lot of help from his father when he started racing.
   c) Lilian didn't like living in England.
   d) Lilian and Ayrton didn't stay together as husband and wife.
   e) Ayrton often crashed his car in Formula Three.
   f) Ayrton won the 1984 Monaco Grand Prix.
   g) Formula One drivers only get points if they come first, second or third.

5 What do you think? Did Senna become a great driver more because of luck or hard work?

CHAPTERS 3–5

Before you read

6 Match the words with the descriptions.

fuel teammate death God helmet

a) This is the opposite of life.
b) If you don't have this, the engine in your car can't work.
c) Christians, Jews and Muslims believe in this person.
d) This goes on your head to keep it safe in an accident.
e) This is a person who works or does sport in the same group as you.

7 The title of Chapter 4 is 'Teammate trouble'. What sort of trouble does Senna have with a teammate, do you think?

After you read

8 Who won the championship in these years?
a) 1988 b) 1989 c) 1990

9 Match the two halves of the sentences.
a) Elio de Angelis
b) Gerhard Berger
c) Alain Prost
e) Ron Dennis
f) Xuxa
g) Jean-Marie Balestre

i) was the head of FISA.
ii) was Senna's girlfriend.
iv) died in a car crash.
v) thought that Senna's driving was dangerous.
vi) was the boss of McLaren.
vii) was Senna's teammate after Prost.

10 Prost or Senna?
a) He never drove faster than he had to.
b) He believed in God.
c) He made a stupid mistake at the 1988 Monaco Grand Prix.
d) He was good friends with Jean-Marie Balestre.
e) He did more exercise than most other drivers.

SELF-STUDY ACTIVITIES

CHAPTERS 6-8

Before you read

11 Guess the answers to these questions. Then read and check.
   a) What did Senna want to do when he stopped racing?
   b) Did he find someone to take Xuxa's place in his life?
   c) Have many Formula One drivers died on the track since Senna?

After you read

12 Choose the correct word.
   a) Senna had trouble with his **gears** / **tyres** in the Brazilian Grand Prix of 1991.
   b) Senna **won** / **didn't win** the 1991 championship.
   c) Senna was **happy** / **unhappy** with his McLaren car in 1992.
   d) He couldn't race for Williams in 1993 because of **Prost** / **Adriane**.
   e) In 1994, Senna was racing for **Williams** / **McLaren**.

13 Answer the questions.
   a) Why did Senna say 'It's going to be a season with lots of accidents.'?
   b) Why did Senna go to the track hospital after his first qualifying laps at San Marino?
   c) Why did Senna have an Austrian flag in his car for the San Marino Grand Prix?
   d) What happened at Tamburello Corner?
   e) Why was Senna's family upset with the bosses of Formula One?
   f) In what ways is Formula One safer now than it was at the time of Senna's death?
   g) Why didn't Bruno Senna race when he was a young teenager?
   h) What is the Ayrton Senna Institute?

14 What do you think? Answer these questions.
   a) Some people thought Senna was a bad example for motor racing. Do you agree? Why / Why not?
   b) Was Senna's accident anyone's fault? Whose?
   c) Would you like to be a Formula One driver? Why / Why not?